CLOUD

CW01265791

'From the CLiPPA-wii comes a second volume of poetry, *Cloud Soup*, illustrated by Elīna Braslina with squiggly, cheerful charm. Both limpidly welcoming and profoundly meaningful, some of these poems, on subjects from weird cakes to good ideas, bodies, dust and Antarctica, will surely stay with their enthralled readers for ever.' *The Guardian*

'She is eloquent and thoughtful and, without striving for effect or reaching for the rhetorical flourish, moves effortlessly from the humdrum to the magical, the everyday to the universal… This is the poet not as show-off entertainer or all-wise seer but as an exemplar, an enviably eloquent and subtle facilitator, who seems to be saying: this is my story, what is yours?' *Books for Keeps*

'A delightful collection of poetry… Uplifting and thought-provoking.' *The Scotsman*

'This is a poet at the height of her powers whose love of language and rhythms combine to dazzling effect… This collection has everything – poems to get discussion flowing, poems just to love for the sound of the words, poems to inspire writing. It is the best kind of book.' *Just Imagine*

OTHER TITLES AVAILABLE FROM THE EMMA PRESS

POETRY COLLECTIONS FOR CHILDREN
Moon Juice, by Kate Wakeling
Wain, by Rachel Plummer
Super Guppy, by Edward van de Vendel,
translated from Dutch by David Colmer
Poems the Wind Blew In, by Karmelo C Iribarren,
translated from Spanish by Lawrence Schimel
My Sneezes Are Perfect, by Rakhshan Rizwan

THEMED POETRY ANTHOLOGIES FOR CHILDREN
Falling Out of the Sky: Poems about Myths and Monsters
Watcher of the Skies: Poems about Space and Aliens
The Head that Wears a Crown: Poems about Kings and Queens
Dragons of the Prime: Poems about Dinosaurs
The Bee Is Not Afraid of Me: A Book of Insect Poems

PICTURE BOOKS FOR CHILDREN
Queen of Seagulls, by Rūta Briede,
translated from Latvian by Elīna Brasliņa
The Dog Who Found Sorrow, by Rūta Briede,
translated from Latvian by Elīna Brasliņa
Bicki-Books 1-12, by various
When It Rains, by Rassi Narika, translated from Indonesian
by Ikhda Ayuning Maharsi Degoul and Emma Wright

POETRY PAMPHLETS FOR ADULTS
Sandsnarl, by Jon Stone
This House, by Rehema Njambi
is, thinks Pearl, by Julia Bird
Pilgrim, by Lisabelle Tay
What the House Taught Us, by Anne Bailey

Cloud Soup

POEMS BY KATE WAKELING

ILLUSTRATED BY
ELĪNA BRASLIŅA

Happy reading!

Kate Wakeling

THE EMMA PRESS

For Mum
(who never once turned into a lion)

THE EMMA PRESS

First published in the UK in 2021 by The Emma Press Ltd.

Reprinted in 2022.

Poems © Kate Wakeling 2021.
Illustrations © Elīna Brasliņa 2021.

All rights reserved.

The right of Kate Wakeling and Elīna Brasliņa to be identified
as the creators of this work has been asserted in accordance
with the Copyright, Designs and Patents Act 1988.

ISBN 978-1-912915-74-3

A CIP catalogue record of this book is available
from the British Library.

Printed and bound in Latvia by Jelgavas Tipogrāfija.

The Emma Press
theemmapress.com
hello@theemmapress.com
Jewellery Quarter,
Birmingham, UK

Supported using public funding by
**ARTS COUNCIL
ENGLAND**

Contents

Some Other Names for Rain

I call you the eyelash rinser
and windowpane racer.

I call you cloud soup.

I call you the tongue tickler,
sock seeper,
hair hassler
and ankle surpriser
(when paired with a passing car).

I call you sky spittle.

I call you leaf polisher.

I call you the pavement drummer
and umbrella summoner.

I call you a brigade of micro water bombs
having a skirmish with the lawn.

I call you the puddle artist
who will only draw circles.

I call you a sprinkle of ocean,
far from home.

Mr Mangle's Beard

Mr Mangle got his beard in a tangle.

His wasn't the sort of beard
that was easy to wrangle.

It got huge.
It got wild.
It got weird, that beard.

It dangled down to Mr Mangle's knees
and made him sneeze.

Then the beard got so bushy
his nose disappeared.

People sneered.

But he persevered,
even when everyone peered and jeered
and volunteered to shear it off.

Mr Mangle thought:
Seeing as it's got so tangled,
maybe I'll do something a bit new-fangled.

So he opened it up as a miniature jungle,
invited in bats, beetles, moths, a canary
to nest in amongst it, all knotty and hairy.

He said: *This is your home.*

And people still sneered at Mr Mangle's big beard,
but never again did he pick up a comb.

Stick Insect

Twig twitcher,
leaf creeper,
nobbly gobbler
of secret greens.

The one with the goggly eyes
whose disguise
relies
on being mostly unsurprising.

Spiny climber,
motionless muncher,
stickler for a really good
stick.

Stem statue,
I salute you.

Weird Cake

I decided to bake a weird cake.

I said: I want this cake to be weird.
I want this cake to be so strange,
so odd,
so bafflingly Unlikely-with-a-capital-*UH?*
that this cake,
this weird cake,
might just change the face of the planet.

So I got to work.

I started off with the standards:
eggs, flour, sugar, bit of butter.

And then I got weird with it.

I wanted this cake to have an uncanny crunch
so I mixed in some dog biscuits,
a burnt crust of toast,
and a tantalising quantity of gravel.

I wanted this cake to be soft in the middle,
so I stirred in dandelion clocks,
some bottom-of-the-pocket fluff,
and, as I whisked,
I whispered some sympathetic stuff to the bowl.

Someone said this cake wouldn't rise,
so I looked them hard in the eye
and added a rubber band,
a rocket blaster
and the elastic from my brother's (newly-washed)
    underpants.

Someone else said it wouldn't be moist.
Cakes being moist is a big deal for a lot of people.
So I made the baby dribble in it
and let a raincloud loose on it
and got a whale to do his best blowhole whoosh
    right by it.

At this point, people were really staring.

Someone said: *That cake doesn't look quite right to me.*
Someone else shook their head and said: *Not in my oven.*

But I didn't need their oven.
I baked it by myself.

And do you know what?

When that cake came out,
it was weird.

It was weird.

Which was exactly the way I wanted it.

Bodies

Bodies, bodies everywhere:
knees and noses, hands and hair,

bodies big and bodies small,
bodies keen on volleyball,

hairy nostrils, lengthy shins,
juicy ear lobes, pointy chins,

straight teeth, no teeth, teeth in braces,
legs that don't like running races,

bushy eyebrows, sturdy knees,
bottoms soft as old settees,

bendy, knobbly, speckled, bony,
hear the body's testimony:

that for every shape and height,
there really is no wrong or right –

just bodies doing what they do,
which is to breathe and fart and chew,

just bodies doing what they do,
and every body's right and true.

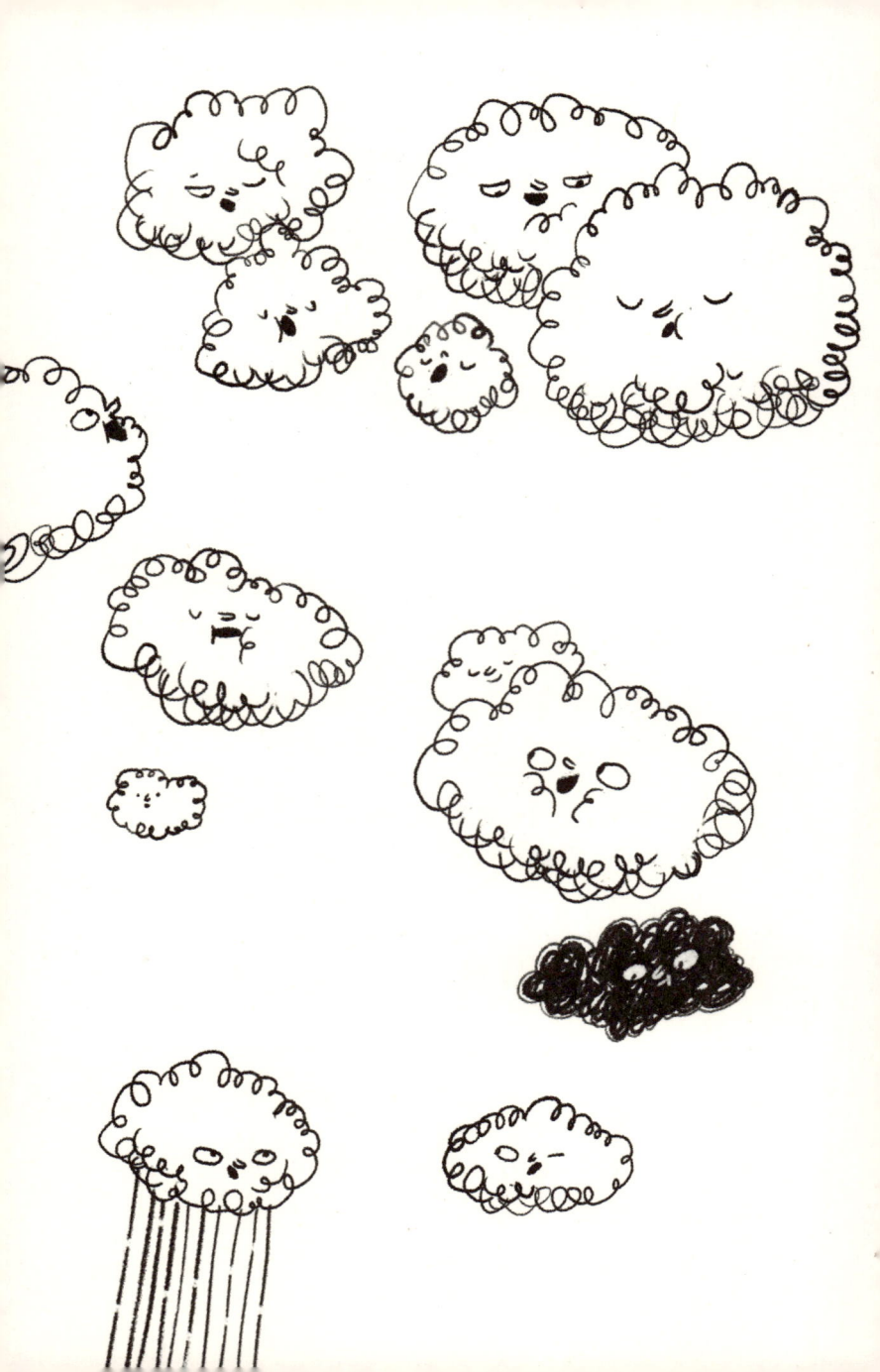

Cloud Song

shy
shape-shifter

misty
whisperer

sky sponge
dabbing at the blue

egg-white
carnival

giant's
duvet

casual teller of slow-mo tales
as whale
becomes boot
becomes flute
becomes a ship with sails

for the world of

        cloud

   is an

    open

book

breathe in
breathe out

   and

     look

The Goblins

Let me tell you of the goblins,
of these foul and wicked sprites,
who creep about on spindly legs
and dish up nasty frights.

They feast on fingers and dead flies,
they sup on curdled milk,
then stroke their goblin bellies
(which are smooth as goblin silk).

They pinch the babies as they sleep
and hang around by bins,
then pass the time by kicking
other goblins on the shins.

They scratch their goblin buttocks
and pick their goblin noses,
then flick their goblin earwax
all across the park's best roses.

And when the day is over
and the goblins head to bed,
they dream their nasty goblin dreams
of wickedness and dread.

So never hobnob with a goblin;
don't let it start a chat:
that goblin'll steal your bus pass
then go and skin the cat.

Paean (or Eleven Uses for a Garden Pea)

1. Frog football.

2. One-third replacement for a miniature traffic light.

3. Temporary emerald for edible ring.

4. Environmentally-friendly clown's nose.

5. Ocean-free planet.

6. False eye for short-sighted lizard.

7. Nostril filler.

8. Spiller of a perfume fresher than newly-mown grass.

9. Cannonball for the Grasshopper Army (THEY'RE COMING).

10. Pesky tester of princesses.

11. Trainee lime.

The water in the glass you are holding right now*

has led a million lives.
It has survived.

Perhaps a splash or two
dashed once or twice
across Niagara Falls.

Or lay locked in the ice
of the first snowball you threw.

Or you'll discover
this water once washed the hands of your
great-great-great grandmother.

Maybe it powered the leaves
of your favourite tree.

* (*Feel free to fetch one.*)

Or once was brewed as tea
or (forgive me)
kangaroo wee.

Perhaps it held the drops
that quenched the thirst
of the very first
triceratops.

Water goes nowhere and everywhere.
Water knows everything.

So it's not such a leap
to think
you hold in your hand
a link
to every kind of wildness,
to every kind of person.

Drink deep.

Toucan

A toucan can,
with that beak,
that brilliant bill,
that multi-coloured whopper on the front of
    its face—
well, a toucan can do anything.

Anything!

OK, not anything.
But *a lot.*
No one is calling this bird a toucan't, right?

So, I bet with this beak of beaks
a toucan can pick locks,
and scratch backs
and provide a slide for thrill-seeking ladybirds.

I bet this bird can dip the tip of its bill
in ink like a quill
and write poems about toucans
(*what's to say this wasn't written by one?*)

and on gloomy days
this beak could be a stand-in rainbow.

But I suppose,
sad to say,
just because a toucan *can*,
doesn't mean it does.

The Deep

Down,
deep down,
where it's deadly dark,
where the ocean shivers black,
where the world is surely all too awful,
there, meet the creatures of the midnight zone.

Meet the creatures who cook their crazy in the cold.

Ghost-eyed,

    razor-grinned,

        milk-skinned,

    silk-finned,

they gulp the gloom,

        they drift and float and creep and cope.

Meet these flukes of the deep,

    secret freaks

    at home

    in the kingdom of the strange.

The School for Ghouls

The school for ghouls
is where ghosts and spooks
learn the tools of the trade.

The ghouls are schooled
in how to go bump in the night,
or perform a LEVEL 7 FRIGHT
by looming weirdly on the stairs in
   the crisp moonlight.

Lessons start at midnight
(unless the clock strikes thirteen).

The ghouls must stick to the rules
for the school's head-
mistress
won't suffer fools.

Note how she carries her head,
(chopped off at the neck)
under one arm.

Oh they say her punishments are
GRAVE.

The ghouls learn chain-rattling,
teeth-chattering
and how to get online with a spider's web.

For the classic white-sheet ghost,
the laundry module is a must.

So, roll up for a term
at the school for ghouls.

Join the creepy crew.

I heard
the spelling tests
only cover one word:

BOO

I, ROBOT

H1

1, R0B0T

S0RRY
KN0W R0B0T WR1T1NG
1S SH0RT 0N W0RDS

[R0B0T B00KS
M0STLY N0T V L0NG]

1 FIND
R0B0T WR1T1NG
ST1LL 0K
W1TH B1T 0F T0-1NG / FR0-1NG

G00D T0 ST1CK T0 P01NT, N0?

S0
TH1S R0B0T 1S L1K1NG:

G0LF
F1SH1NG
PH1L0S0PHY
Z00MING T0 M00NS 1S 0K T00
~~W1P1NG N0N-R0B0TS 0FF TH1S~~
~~W0RLD 1N W1LD R0B0T V1CT0RY~~

T1P T0P M1X 0F R0B0T TH1NGS

0K TH1NK 1T 1S N0W G0 0'CL0CK F0R
TH1S R0B0T
W1SH1NG J0Y BL1SS THR1LLS T0
R0B0TS/N0N-R0B0TS B0TH

S0 L0NG

To the Last Dinosaur Standing

Because there had to be *one*, who watched the world sizzle and crack as it faced that almighty meteor THWACK (it seems we're sure this is the fixture that finished them off). There had to be *one* who saw skies thicken with black, who watched the wilt of every shred of green, who trod through dust to seek a last curled leaf, or gnawed upon some final bit of dino-beef. And it must have been a horrible happening, that sink from life, that sudden stop to the business of being a dinosaur.

And so I hail that beast whose heart ticked on the extra hour, who sighed and stood upon the shadowed ground before it took its endmost gulp. I salute you, whichever cool-blooded soul it was who came to be the last to go, whose tiny walnut brain must have meant (I only hope) that of its lonely fate, it could not know.

I am looking at this painting called Blue Circus *by Marc Chagall*

and my eyes start to swim.

I look
and I look
and the next thing I know,
my feet are floating clean off the ground

and I'm up there:
I'm in it.

I'm swooping through a blue
so deep
so soft
so true
I can taste it.

Here is the tumbler in blazing red,
her toes just missing the tip of my nose.

Here is the horse

(who's green, of course),
his breath now warm on my wrists.

Here is the moon and fiddle,
the rooster and drum.

Here is the circus clatter,
its clunk, swish and hum.

Ah yes, and here is the fish,
the fish with the flowers.

But wait a second,
how is that fish *actually*—
I mean,
is it holding the flowers with its *fin*
or does it have some kind of fishy
    hand of fingers?

And no sooner do I ask the question then
snap
I'm back where I started,
feet flat to the earth.

Tight behind the glass of the frame,
the circus swirls on without me

but the taste
of that deep deep blue
stays sweet on my tongue.

Why Good Ideas Might Also Be a Bit Like Moths

Because both hatch from tiny and unlikely eggs.

Because they mostly dwell in darkness,
fluttering just out of reach
before a light clicks
on and they hurtle
into view.

Because handle them too roughly
and they dissolve to dust.

Because open all your windows,
switch on all your lamps,
wait,

and one will come.

13 Slippery Facts about Antarctica

1. Antarctica is covered in ice a mile thick.

2. There are no trees, polar bears or rainy days on Antarctica.

3. There are no hamsters, jokes or salt and vinegar crisps there either.

4. If all the ice in Antarctica were to melt, sea levels would rise by 60m.

5. That's about the height of 14 double-decker buses.

6. (There are no double-decker buses on Antarctica.)

7. If you place an ear to the ground there, you will hear the ice creak and sigh with worry.

8. Antarctica is actually a desert.

9. And if you were to spatter raspberry syrup and chocolate sprinkles over a small circle of the ice there, Antarctica would also (technically) be a dessert.

10. In March 2000, an iceberg called B-15 broke off Antarctica and melted into the ocean.

11. This iceberg was the size of Jamaica.

12. Buried deep in Antarctica are lakes and mountain peaks all covered by ice.

13. Buried deep in Antarctica is a missing brain cell, apparently lost by the human race some years ago. This lost brain cell is at last, let's hope, beginning to thaw.

Numbers 1, 2, 4, 5, 6, 8, 10, 11 and 12 are true. Number 9 is (technically) true too. Number 3 probably isn't. As for numbers 7 and 13: your guess is as good as mine.

Grandma and the Sea

One winter, my grandma wasn't very well
and I ended up staying with her for Christmas.

Just me and Grandma.

I knew she wouldn't be here much longer.
Her back crackled with pain
and her thoughts had loosened like the strands of
wool in a well-worn scarf.

Christmas Day came and it was a cold day.
A grey-washed,
iron-toothed sort of day.

We were pretty miserable.

Now, my grandma lived by the sea
but she couldn't get to the beach any more.

And I can't remember if it was me or Grandma
who cooked it up,
but we agreed I should go for a swim.

We would give this cold grey Christmas Day
a run for its money.

So, I made my way to the beach,
just me,
and I stamped on into the water.

And *by heck* it was cold.
A huge, wild cold
that hit me like a bus.

The water tumbled and roared,
and anger flew round me:
that my grandma might not live much more,
that she now found her days
too long,
too short.

And then,
just as fast,
the crash of that mad grey sea
walloped me to gladness,
for her kindness and quickness,
for her fierceness,
for all the time we'd had.

And I came home and told my grandma
I'd done it,
I'd swum in that stupidly cold water
and she grinned,
her cheeks beaming pink as mine.

And now my grandma
isn't here anymore.

And it's sad.

But when I'm near a cold sea
I make sure to think of her.

I think about the glitter and sting of salt water.

And I swim in it.

Just Dust

What *are* those dusty bits and bobs
that float about
and twist and sway
when sunshine
strikes them in a certain way?

It'd be nice, I suppose,
to think of them as specks of dreams, say,
or flecks of broken stars
or fairy gold
or the silvery scales of mystic fishes
or worn-out wishes.

But no, I think they're nothing more
than dust and fluff,
scraps of cobweb,
dirt and other useless stuff.

Yes, they're ordinary as toast and socks.

But perhaps I like them all the more for this.

Much better these bits of nothingness,
the forgotten and the thrown-away,
are made so magic
simply by the light of day.

The Absolutely Worst Food in the World

The absolutely worst food in the world
is of course _____.*

This is beyond discussion.

I revolt against _____
with every fibre of my being.

Because there's just something
fundamentally wrong about _____.

The texture.
The smell.
(Don't get me started on the smell.)

I 100% do not trust the look of it either.

Give me _____ and I will say:
I'd rather eat my own toenails.
I'd rather eat your *toenails.*

* *Insert foodstuff of your choice.*

And I will almost mean it.

All I'm asking
is that we fling the lot of it into a volcano.

Or better yet:
package it up,
find a rocket
and blast every last mouthful of
＿＿＿＿＿＿＿＿ into deep space.

Because the absolutely worst food in the world
is of course ＿＿＿＿＿＿＿＿
and it is high time
someone did something about it.

The Flibbit

Here's the thing about the flibbit,
as it's time someone explained:
she's quick as light and light as air,
with mischief on the brain.

When you're sitting somewhere solemn
and it's crucial you don't sneeze,
she's what tickles at your nostrils
(with her small and knobbly knees).

Or if you've put your shoes on
and are ready to step out
but find an itch between your toes,
well, reader, have no doubt:

it's the flibbit, yes the flibbit,
minor mayhem is her mission,
she's the overlord of awkward,
irritation's top magician.

That tingle on your scalp you get
when someone mentions nits?
Mull no more, for in your hair
a certain someone sits.

It's the flibbit, yes the flibbit,
who is fiddling with your follicles,
this flibbit loves the whipping up
of just such little obstacles.

She's Ninja of the Niggle,
the nano nag you can't ignore,
but take note: her naughty knack
is only nuisance, nothing more.

So if you find yourself in trouble
for a fretful sort of fidget,
remember just to answer:
NOT MY FAULT, IT WAS THE FLIBBIT.

I Just Have a Few Questions

after Matthew Welton

So how long do you think it's been living
in your rucksack?

Is this fog or something far more sinister?

Wouldn't that be easier with a spoon?

Have you always been nervous around
goats or was there a specific incident?

Are you sure that's definitely a
toothbrush?

Did you forget about the pirates again?

Shall we just leave it where we found it
and say no more about it?

Who told you that satsuma was cursed?

Why are they still talking about how
messy this room is?

What if it *wasn't* all a dream?

Could you say that again but this time in a
  whisper?

Is it just me or can everyone see the large
  floating door with pale blue light coming
  out of it?

Why is it still Wednesday?

What are we going to do about the lizards?

The Poem Says No

The poem says no.

The poem says it can't
it won't
it hasn't
it isn't
it doesn't
and it is very very very unlikely ever to.

The poem says nope, nada, nil, nay, no way,
not today.

Not to put too fine a point on it
the poem would prefer not to.

And it (the poem) would also like the last
word on this
which is:

no.

In Praise of the Guinea Pig

All hail the hairy one without a tail.

Not mini, not big,
you, guinea pig,
are pretty regular all-round.

And your rump is, well,
all round too.

Sure, you don't do funny tricks.
But you make those little chatters and clicks
and scuttle about with your unexpectedly
   furry babies.

I'll admit you haven't the sharpest of wits
and, despite your hairy rosettes,
you're not the most glamorous of pets.

Not sleek as a cat,
not quick as a rat,
you're no puppy or pony or parrot.

But I love that you're just really really
happy with a lump of

                              carrot.

Wardrobe Monkeys

The wardrobe monkeys are one-foot high.
They lunch on dust and play *I spy*.

The wardrobe monkeys like warm houses
and (when bored) try on your trousers.

They're shy as shadows, meek as moles,
they dart about like pond tadpoles,

so trust you'll never catch a glimpse
of these hush-hush cupboard chimps,

but know that nothing dark's occurring
should you hear a monkey stirring:

yawning, scratching, twiddling ear lobes,
is what monkeys do in wardrobes.

The Day Mum Turned into a Lion

The day Mum turned into a lion
was not a good day.

I suppose we were being *difficult*:
bit of this, bit of that,
a spat involving the sofa,
some orange squash,
the cat.

Mum got cross.

Tired after work,
voice gone hard,
we'd *really gone and done it now.*

And as she left the room,
shoulders shaking,
I glimpsed a flash of fur,
a claw.

Her footsteps thudded heavy in the hall
then came a roar.

We ran to look and there she was,

a lion.

Huge, gold,
eyes ablaze.

She gazed at us,
opened her jaws
and we saw the glinting tips of her teeth.

She growled
and the ground shook under our feet.

Then she was off,
prowling through the house,
tail slamming doors,
paws swiping washing all over the floor.

She swept upstairs,
leapt on the bed,
turned to the sky
and roared and roared and roared.

We watched, trembling.

I held my brother's hand.

Then she stopped,
turned and saw us.

And my mum the lion
put that huge golden head of hers to one side,
smiled a toothy smile,
and yawned.

She nudged past me
to pad to my room
and curl up on my bed.

And in an instant she was asleep,
nose tucked deep into her tail.

She looked so soft, so still,
purring like an engine,
fur warm as sunlight,
that we clambered up beside her.

And when we all woke up
my mum the lion
was just my mum again.

She touched us each on the cheek,
mouthed *sorry*
and we did the same.

We all tidied up
and no one said a word.

Word Hoard

Long ago,
when people laid straw on their floors,
and played football with pigs' bladders
and stuck leeches on the legs of the sick –
long *long* ago –
well, they made word hoards.

A word hoard is a set of words
with a certain magic about them.
They're words that stir the spirit
and tingle on the tongue.

A word hoard is a secret stash of vocab
that makes your heart hum.

Now, you might like a word
for its sound
or for its sense.

Or you might like a word
for both its music and its meaning,
like… *picnic* perhaps?

In any case, what you put in your word hoard
  is up to you.

Here's mine:

quick	tendril	magic	feast
root	music	weird	fierce
thirst	blossom	curse	drift
bright	worm	wander	sleep

What words,
I wonder,
might you keep
in yours?

The Day of Silence

Nyepi is an important day on the island of Bali that happens once a year. It is a day of complete quiet when everybody stays at home, preferably with the curtains closed, no music playing and no lights on. Evil spirits are believed to pass over the island during Nyepi, but on finding everything so quiet they are fooled into thinking Bali is deserted and so fly away.

You may of course read out this poem at any volume of your choosing, but I strongly recommend you whisper it.

hear the hush
of held breath

finger to lips
shut the door

and wait
for the demon

eclipse
as spirits

swoop by
to swarm

the sky
with spook

don't laugh
don't shout

don't speak
don't speak

just hope
you win

this epic
game

of hide
and seek

Bad Dream Poem

and that table over there is actually the
whole of Norway. And on the ceiling is
the next-door neighbour's cat. But the cat
is in fact my first ever teacher. Hi Mrs
Dolman. And now we're in a fairground.
Of course we are. And there are some
people without faces plus my old friend
Angie who I've not thought about for
maybe a hundred years. Hi Angie. Oh
and here's my cousin wearing – yes, this
is all making more sense – a suit of
armour that makes a noise like a very
very distant electric guitar. And the
armour has these flags on that I think
make people burst into flames if they lick
them? That part's a big deal. And
suddenly we're all dancing with these
horribly complicated steps and it's very
important for *the koalas* that we get them
right because, well, everybody knows
why. And I do seem to be struggling with

the footwork. This isn't good. This isn't good at all. Especially when I'm wearing – a wetsuit plus really heavy shoes? And I'm also meant to be taking the Seventy-sixth Matchstick Exam. And all my pens are made of pastry. And the clock is actually a fish tank. And I'm sitting on my own in a huge room that is also the cupboard where we used to keep the

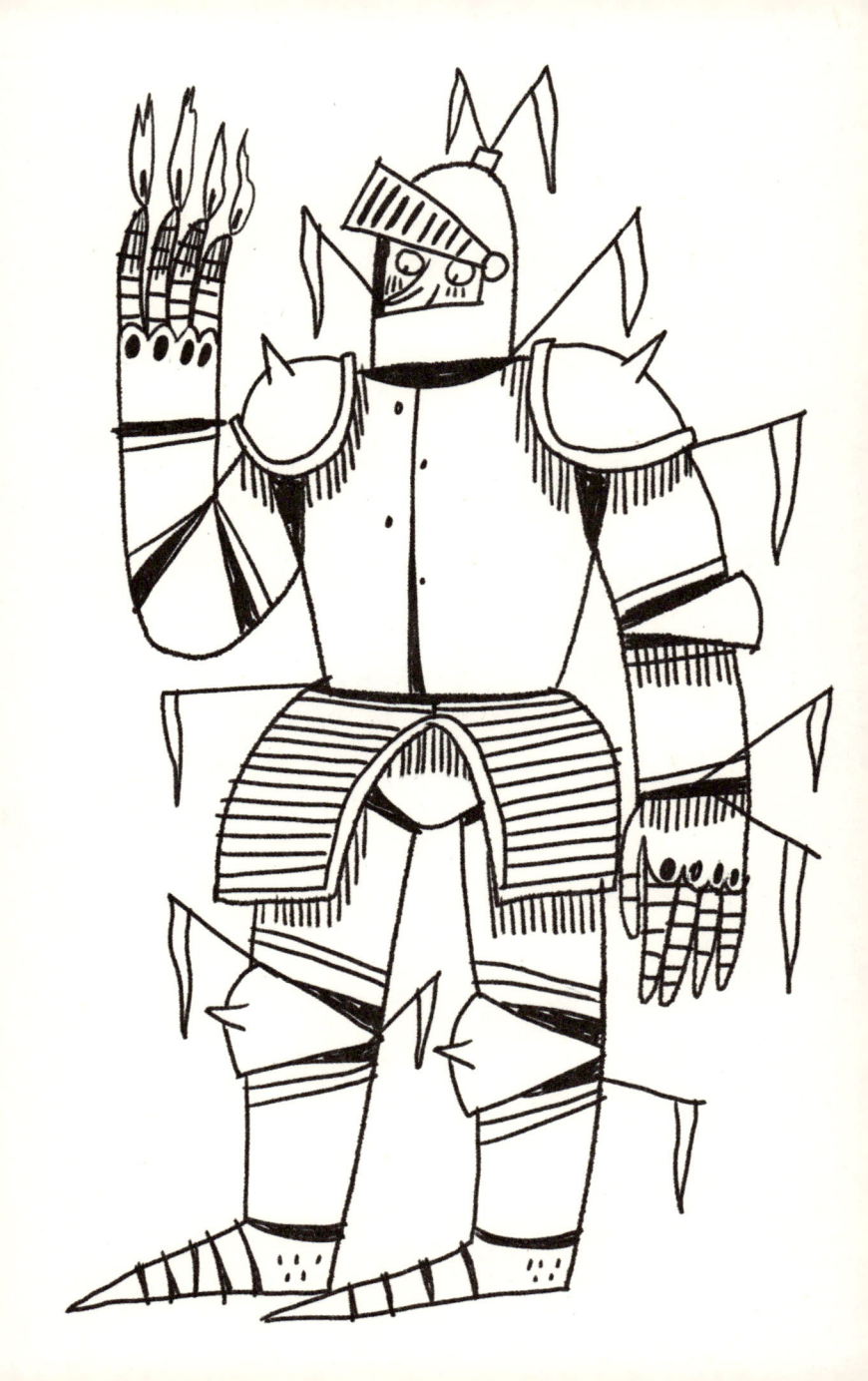

XII
to stop the
skull clock
and its

XI
I can
but oh tonight
it is tricky

X
learn not to
wind its cogs
I can

IX
I know
I can stop
this clock

VIII
hours
it says
will come

VII
it murmurs
of the
anxious

The Skull Clock

I
tick tock
tick tock
the skull clock

II
knocks
at my brain
its pendulum

III
swings fat
with worry
its chimes

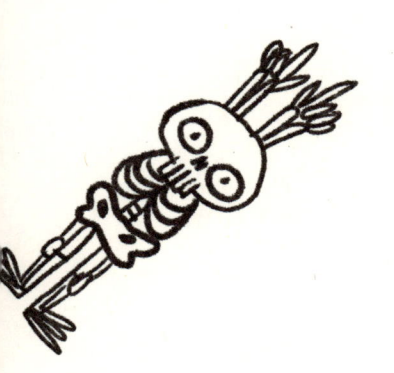

IV
keep me
waking
waking

V
it whispers me
back
to the old

VI
minutes
of the day
just gone

Walking Poem

after Theodore Roethke

When the brain is clogged and slow
or lost and low,
I take to my feet.

I walk my troubles loose.

heel to toe
heel to toe

I walk my thoughts.

I walk them through until they flow,
I do not slow.

I let my walking set my thinking free.

For in my feet, I put my trust:
I let them leave my worries
far behind,

like footprints in the dust.

I do not run.

heel to toe
heel to toe

I let the answers come,
I let the questions go.

I walk until I find my path.

heel to toe
heel to toe

I walk to find out where I need to go.

The Baddies: A Miscellany

Vipers Val

The Ancient Guzzlejax of Golanjibub

Stinking Gary the Ghoul

The Thing Under the Bed with the Horrible Eyes

Kimberley Crocker the Crooked Kitten Cooker

Old Yellowtooth the Biter

The Skullbot Terror-Droid 5000

Thumpeldush the Mighty Ogre of Ozgud

Peaches Glitz and her Dazzling Demon Horde

_____, the Unspeakable.

Archibald Toadmouth III, Baron of the Ruinous Swamp

T H E   C L A W

Spidery Dave

Nose Can Do

My nose knows all sorts.

My nose knows roses and toes
before my eyes spy them.

(This knowing about toes
is one of the nose's woes.)

My nose knows
because it's composed of two small Os
that don't close.

My nose knows *more* than my elbows
but *less* than a rhino's nose,
which is fine, I suppose.

My nose knows quite enough.

Unless it's full of stuff
and needs a blow
in which case
my nose knows nothing at all
and may as well be a potato with a couple
   of holes drilled in it.

But let's not get bogged down in this.

My nose knows what it knows.

Tree

Take heart in tree.

Take heart in this large friend
who is fixed and brings colour and cool

        and sometimes ants.

(But don't worry about the ants.
The ants are OK.)

Take heart in tree because tree knows
how to drink sunshine.

Tree knows the meaning of roots
and the way to sift the dirt,
find its sweetness
then set aside the rest.

Tree breathes.

Tree chimes its green.

Tree lets others come and go,
knows when to wait
and when to grow.

Tree takes its space.

Take heart in tree.

Free

and we will open all the doors
and we will jump on all the beds
and we will leap from mountain top to mountain top
and we will laugh until we think we might explode
and we will laugh especially in those moments when we aren't supposed to
and we will of course find this only makes the laughing a million times
    more extreme
and we will talk to animals
and we will stride across oceans
and we will dance like maniacs
and we will lie on the sofa watching TV with our shoes on because why not

and we will have long baths/short baths/no baths delete as applicable
and we will eat delicious foods
and we will not eat any of the bits we don't really like
and we will talk while lying on our backs and looking at the sky
and we will say the first thing that pops into our heads
and we will be always with our friends even when we are not
and we will smile with smiles so deep they make our eyes disappear
and we will grow wings
and we will
and we will
and we will

NOW WRITE YOUR OWN POEM!

Here are some ideas from editor Emma Wright to get you started...

Did Kate's poem 'Weird Cake' (page 8) make you want to bake a weird cake of your own? What would you put in it? Write a list of the most satisfying colours, textures, tastes, smells and sounds you can think of, and then write a poem about your cake. Make sure you include the best combination of things from your list!

 This book is called *Cloud Soup*, so you should definitely write a poem about clouds. If the sun isn't too bright, look up at the sky and examine the clouds. What do they look like? Can you spot any interesting shapes? Do they remind you of anything, like in the poem on page 15? Write down your observations and put them into poem titled 'A Guide to the Sky'.

'Grandma and the Sea' on page 47 is a story poem, telling us very vividly about a particular time and place. Is there a moment that you have a very strong memory of, because of how intense your feelings were at the time? It could be your first day of school, or a birthday, or something else entirely!

Write a poem that tells this as a story, explaining what happened and why you still remember it now. Try to help the reader imagine they were there too – what details can you include to help them picture it exactly?

On page 54 you'll find a poem that is just waiting for you to fill in the spaces: 'The Absolutely Worst Food in the World'. Copy it out and write in your choice of the Worst Food (mine is tomatoes), and then read it out to someone who really *needs* to know. You could make it into a performance, with actions to go along with the words!

Pick a line that intrigues you from 'I Just Have a Few Questions' on page 59. Who do you think is asking that question? What do you think has happened or is happening to them? Pretend you are this person and write a poem in their voice. You could write it very clearly, to explain the situation, or you could be more mysterious.

Do you have a favourite animal? Kate writes about the guinea pig on page 65, describing all the ways a guinea pig is great and why it's quite funny too. Write a poem in praise of your favourite animal, including all the little details about it that make it special.

ABOUT THE AUTHOR

Kate Wakeling is a poet and musicologist. Her debut poetry collection for children, *Moon Juice*, won the CLiPPA in 2017 and was nominated for the Carnegie Medal.

Kate's poetry for adults has been published widely, including in the *Guardian*, *The Forward Book of Poetry* 2016 (Faber & Faber) and *The Best British Poetry 2014* (Salt). Kate studied music at Cambridge University and holds a PhD in Balinese gamelan music from the School of Oriental & African Studies.

Kate lives in Oxford with her family, which includes two small children and any number of wardrobe monkeys.

You can visit Kate's website and see more of her poems here: www.katewakeling.co.uk

ABOUT THE ILLUSTRATOR

 Elīna Braslia studied Printmaking and Graphic Arts at the Art Academy of Latvia. Since 2014 she has illustrated more than twenty titles, including *Moon Juice* by Kate Wakeling, which was her international debut. She has been nominated for numerous awards in Latvia, and has won the Zelta Ābele (Golden Apple Tree) National Prize for Book Art four times. She was awarded the International Jānis Baltvilks Prize in 2017.

You can visit Elīna's website and see more of her illustrations here: www.elinabraslina.com

ABOUT THE EMMA PRESS

The Emma Press is an independent publishing house based in the Jewellery Quarter, Birmingham, UK. It was founded in 2012 by Emma Dai'an Wright, and specialises in poetry, short fiction and children's books.

In 2020 The Emma Press received funding from Arts Council England's Elevate programme, developed to enhance the diversity of the arts and cultural sector by strengthening the resilience of diverse-led organisations.

You can find out more about The Emma Press and buy books here:

Website: theemmapress.com
Facebook @theemmapress
Twitter: @theemmapress
Instagram: @theemmapress

My Sneezes Are Perfect

Poems by Rakhshan Rizwan, with Yusuf Samee
Illustrated by Benjamin Phillips

What's your favourite food? Who's your best friend?
Have you tried to grow a rock? Aren't beards weird?
Did you ever move house and miss your old home?
Didn't a lot change when the pandemic started?

My Sneezes Are Perfect is a collection of poems in
the voice of a small boy who wants to tell you about
all the things he's learning, all the time. During the
book, he moves from the Netherlands to America
and has to adjust to his new life there. Then
Covid-19 hits and his world changes all over again...

Paperback ISBN 978-1-912915-68-2
Poems aimed at children aged 8+